WELCOME TO MY COUNTRY

Welcome to
NEW ZEALAND

Gareth Stevens Publishing
A WORLD ALMANAC EDUCATION GROUP COMPANY

Written by
DORA YIP/AYESHA ERCELAWN

Edited in USA by
ALAN WACHTEL

Designed by
JAILANI BASARI

Picture research by
SUSAN JANE MANUEL

First published in North America in 2002 by
Gareth Stevens Publishing
A World Almanac Education Group Company
330 West Olive Street, Suite 100
Milwaukee, Wisconsin 53212 USA

Please visit our web site at:
www.garethstevens.com
For a free color catalog describing
Gareth Stevens' list of high-quality books
and multimedia programs, call
1-800-542-2595 (USA) or
1-800-461-9120 (CANADA).
Gareth Stevens Publishing's
Fax: (414) 332-3567.

© **TIMES MEDIA PRIVATE LIMITED 2002**
Originated and designed by
Times Editions
an imprint of Times Media Private Limited
Times Centre, 1 New Industrial Road
Singapore 536196
http://www.timesone.com.sg/te

Library of Congress Cataloging-in-Publication Data
Yip, Dora.
Welcome to New Zealand / Dora Yip and Ayesha Ercelawn.
p. cm.—(Welcome to my country)
Includes bibliographical references and index.
Summary: An overview of the geography, history, government,
economy, people, and culture of New Zealand.
ISBN 0-8368-2532-2 (lib. bdg.)
1. New Zealand—Juvenile literature. [1. New Zealand.]
I. Ercelawn, Ayesha. II. Title. III. Series.
DU408.Y57   2002
993—dc21   2001042015

Printed in Malaysia

1 2 3 4 5 6 7 8 9 06 05 04 03 02

PICTURE CREDITS
ANA Press Agency: 19
Archive Photos: 31 (top)
Susanna Burton: 1, 20, 25, 43
Camera Press: 29 (right)
Helen Ough Dealy: 44
Focus Team – Italy: 40
Lee Foster: 9 (bottom)
Haga Library, Japan: 38
HBL Network Photo Agency: 34, 36
Dave G. Houser: 18 (top), 33
Hutchison Library: 3 (bottom), 26
Nazima Kowall: 3 (top), 12, 28 (top)
Life File Photo Library: 8
North Wind Picture Archives: 10,
    11 (bottom)
NZTB: Cover, 45
Christine Osborne Pictures: 7,
    18 (bottom), 41
David Simson: 3 (center), 21, 23, 37
Topham Picturepoint: 4, 5, 11 (top),
    13, 14, 15 (bottom), 16, 29 (left),
    31 (bottom)
Trip Photo Library: 2, 6, 9 (top), 17, 22,
    24, 27, 28 (bottom), 30, 32, 35, 39
Vision Photo Agency/Hulton Getty: 15 (top)

Digital Scanning by Superskill Graphics Pte Ltd

Most New Zealanders live on North Island where the capital city, Wellington, is located. North Island has many large volcanoes. Lake Taupo, New Zealand's largest lake, is actually an ancient volcanic **crater**. South Island has a more rugged **terrain** with spectacular **glaciers**, mountains, and **fjords**. New Zealand's highest peak is Mount Cook. It is 12,349 feet (3,764 meters) high. Australia is New Zealand's nearest large neighbor.

Above: Because Mount Cook is so high, the Maori call it *Aoraki,* which means "cloud piercer." Mount Cook is on South Island.

Climate

New Zealand has a mild and moist climate. Because the country lies south of the equator, the islands' warmest months are January and February. July is its coldest month.

Rain falls a lot more in the western part of New Zealand than in the eastern part. Most years, the country gets more rain in winter than in summer.

Plants and Animals

Since New Zealand is so far away from other land, most of its native plants cannot be found anywhere else! The country's plants include many evergreens, such as kauri trees and tree ferns, which have leaves all year round.

Among New Zealand's native animals are flightless birds, such as the well-known kiwi and the world's largest flightless parrot, the kakapo. When settlers arrived, they brought along animals such as rats, cats, and dogs that now threaten these birds.

Above: The kaka beak (*Clianthus puniceus*) is a native plant once common in the wild. It is now found mainly in gardens.

Left: The kiwi, named for its call "ki-wi," is New Zealand's national symbol. This bird is now an endangered species because of **predators** and the loss of its **habitat**.

History

The Maori have lived in New Zealand since at least the ninth century. When they arrived, their main food was a tall, flightless bird called a moa. Over time, the moa was hunted to **extinction**. The Maori also grew taro, a vegetable they brought with them from Polynesia.

Below: In the 1700s, Europeans came to New Zealand to hunt whales for their oil.

The First Europeans

In 1642, a Dutch sailor, Abel Tasman, was the first European to discover New Zealand. His crew tried to land, but the Maori killed some of them. The Dutch named the islands "Nieuw Zeeland," after a province in the Netherlands.

In 1769, Captain James Cook, a British navigator, landed on North Island. He made friends with the Maori and explored the two main islands. Before long, Europeans came to settle and trade in New Zealand.

Above: After the Maori killed some of Tasman's crew, no Europeans tried to land in New Zealand until 1769.

Below: Captain James Cook, a British explorer, made maps of North and South Islands.

War and Colonization

After the settlers and the Maori began trading, the Maori fought tribal wars with guns they got from the settlers. Many Maori died in the wars, as well as from diseases brought by settlers.

On February 6, 1840, New Zealand became a British colony, when the British governor and the Maori chiefs signed the Treaty of Waitangi. This treaty protected Maori rights and promised that Maori land would be sold only to the British.

Above:
Railroads built in New Zealand in the late 1800s helped businesses grow.

As more British settlers arrived, they demanded more and more land. Many Maoris did not want to sell their land, so land wars broke out. Although Maori tribes united under one king in 1858, they lost most of their land in the wars between 1850 and 1870.

Left: The Maori tribal wars ended in the 1830s, when the Maori realized they were killing their own race. This nineteenth-century Maori warrior is dressed for battle.

Colonial History

The British colony grew quickly. Soon, the settlers wanted to run their own government. By 1852, New Zealand had its own constitution.

New Zealand's economy boomed as farmers began exporting wool, dairy products, and meat to Britain and other European countries.

The people of New Zealand were proud of their colony and thought of themselves as a separate nation. In 1947, New Zealand gained almost complete independence from Britain.

Left: When gold was discovered on South Island in the 1860s, **prospectors** from as far away as the United States rushed to New Zealand.

Abel Tasman (1603–1659)

Dutch explorer Abel Tasman was the first European to discover New Zealand. The next European to arrive was Captain James Cook, but not until 127 years later.

Abel Tasman

Potatau Te Wherowhero (1800–1860)

Potatau Te Wherowhero, a chief of the Waikato, was crowned Maori king in 1858. He worked to protect his people's rights to their land. Today, Maori leaders continue to work for the rights of their people.

Sir George Grey

Sir George Grey (1812–1898)

Sir George Grey was governor of New Zealand from 1845 to 1853 and from 1861 to 1868. He had great respect for the Maori and wrote about their **mythology**. He also helped write New Zealand's constitution.

Government and the Economy

New Zealand has a parliamentary form of government. The British monarch is the official head of state but does not have much power. The prime minister is the head of Parliament.

Citizens who are eighteen years or older vote to elect the Parliament's 120 members. Each member serves a

Below: Cabinet ministers meet in the "Beehive," one of the government buildings in the city of Wellington.

three-year term. The National Party and the Labour Party are the two main political parties in Parliament. The leader of the party with the most members in Parliament becomes the prime minister of New Zealand.

The prime minister appoints a cabinet of ministers to run government departments. The prime minister and the cabinet can propose **bills**, but the members of Parliament must vote for a bill before it can become a law.

Farming

Farming is big business in New Zealand. The country's mild climate and frequent rainfall are ideal for growing crops and raising livestock.

New Zealand's main exports are meat, dairy products, passionfruit, tamarillos, and kiwifruit. Some of New Zealand's unusual fruits have become popular all over the world. Britain, the United States, Australia, Japan, and the Middle East are New Zealand's biggest trading partners.

Above: Kiwifruit has been one of New Zealand's important export crops since the 1970s.

Below: Deer products from New Zealand farms are exported to Europe and Asia.

Industry

New Zealand has a thriving timber industry. Most of its wood is grown on plantations rather than cut down from forests.

Tourism is also an important industry. New Zealand's scenery attracts millions of visitors yearly.

Products made in New Zealand's factories include textiles, plastics, leather goods, and farm machinery.

Above: Tourists can take a harbor cruise in Auckland, the largest city in New Zealand.

People and Lifestyle

New Zealand has a small population of about 3.8 million people, and its culture is very European. About 75 percent of its people are of European **descent**. Their ancestors came from England, Scotland, and Ireland, as well as from many other European countries.

About 15 percent of New Zealand's people are Asians and **immigrants** from other Pacific Islands.

Left: The evening meal is often the only time that New Zealand families get together.

and schooling, many students go on to college. New Zealand has eight major universities and about twenty-five **polytechnics**, with a total of more than 200,000 students at these schools.

Maori children can attend special groups called *te kohanga reo* (teh koh-HAH-nyah RREH-oh). These groups teach Maori language and culture and help preserve the Maori identity.

Religion

Religion does not play a big role in the lives of New Zealanders, and the country has no official religion. About 60 percent of the people are Christian. The rest belong to minority religions or to no religious group.

Early Maori believed all things had a life force or spirit. They prayed to the gods of the mountains, the sky, the sea, and other parts of nature. These gods were important in Maori mythology.

Christian missionaries **converted** many Maori in the 1800s, but during the land wars of the 1860s, some new Maori religions appeared. The first of these was Hauhauism, which became popular on North Island. It combined Jewish, Christian, and traditional Maori beliefs. Another nineteenth-century religion, Ringatu, still has thousands of members. In the 1920s, some Maori joined the Ratana Church, which believes in healing through prayer and faith.

Opposite: Christchurch Cathedral is one of the best known churches in New Zealand.

Language

English and Maori are the two official languages of New Zealand. Before the Europeans arrived, Maori was the only language spoken. Today, most New Zealanders speak English, but many also speak Maori.

Above: This Maori woman is reciting Maori poetry at a marae. People speak only in Maori at some of the tribal meeting houses.

In 1987, the government set up the Maori Language Commission to encourage the daily use of Maori, and this language is now taught in schools and universities. Maori phrases, such as *kia ora* (kee-ah OH-rrah), meaning "hello," and *haere mai* (hay-REH mah-EE), meaning "welcome," and words, such as *pakeha,* are used frequently throughout New Zealand.

Traditionally, Maori poems, songs, and stories were memorized and taught by one generation to the next. Since the **advent** of the Internet, the Maori language and Maori folktales have become more widely known.

Above: This version of the 1840 Treaty of Waitangi is written in the Maori language.

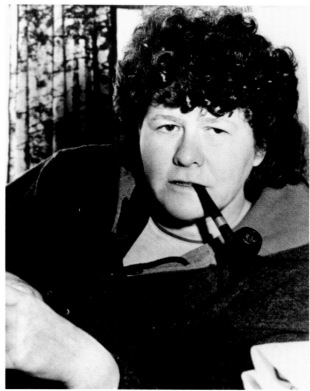

Literature

New Zealand authors often write about their country and culture. Katherine Mansfield (1888–1923) wrote stories set in nineteenth-century New Zealand.

Famous living writers include Keri Hulme, who wrote *The Bone People*, a well-known, award-winning novel, and Margaret Mahy, who writes books for children. Witi Ihimaera is a famous Maori short-story writer.

Above: Katherine Mansfield (*left*) is known for short stories inspired by her early years in Wellington. Today, Keri Hulme (*right*) is one of New Zealand's most famous writers.

Arts

New Zealand has a lively arts scene. A government organization called Creative New Zealand funds many arts, including theater, dance, and opera.

Wellington is known for its theaters. It is also the home of the New Zealand Symphony and the New Zealand Ballet. Dunedin, the country's music capital, is home to several successful rock bands.

Left: The Auckland Art Gallery displays art from all over the world. Shown here is "Seated Figure" by Henry Moore (1898–1986), an English sculptor.

Left:
Jane Campion is New Zealand's best-known film director. Her most famous movie, *The Piano* (1993), is set in the pioneer days of New Zealand.

Famous New Zealand Artists

Frances Hodgkins (1869–1947) was the first painter from New Zealand to become well-known around the world. Famous opera singer Kiri Te Kanawa, who has Maori roots, is from Gisborne. Jane Campion directs award-winning movies. Sam Neill, Russell Crowe, Lucy Lawless, and Anna Paquin are popular actors and actresses from New Zealand who star in movies and television programs.

Above:
Anna Paquin won the Oscar for Best Supporting Actress in 1993 for her part in *The Piano*. She is one of the youngest actors to receive an Academy Award.

Maori Dance

The Maori today still do traditional dances. Men do the *haka* (HAH-kah), which are war dances and chants traditionally performed before battle. They shake clubs or spears, stomp their feet, and stick out their tongues in a threatening way. Women do the *poi* (poh-EE), or ball dance, twirling balls on strings while fluttering their hands and singing and chanting.

Other Maori Art Forms

Carving, weaving, and other traditional arts are taught in many Maori meeting houses. Carved wooden figures decorate some of these meeting houses. Canoes, tools, and jewelry are carved with Maori designs of curving lines and spirals. Maori-style designs can be found all over New Zealand. The symbol of Air New Zealand, the country's airline, is Maori-influenced. Modern Maori artists mix traditional styles with new ideas.

Below: A Maori craftsman at the Maori Arts and Crafts Institute in Rotorua carves symbolic designs into a wooden panel. These carvings often tell a story.

Leisure

Tramping, or hiking, is a popular outdoor activity in New Zealand's many wilderness areas. Hiking trails often run through national parks and past scenic and historic sites.

Mountain areas are popular for skiing and climbing. Peaks such as Cook and Ruapehu are a challenge for most mountain climbers. Some New Zealanders prefer sailing or fishing.

Below: Climbers in the Southern Alps, on South Island, are rewarded with breathtaking views.

Team Sports

Rugby, cricket, soccer, and hockey are popular team sports in New Zealand. Both rugby and cricket were brought to New Zealand by the British. Rugby is the country's favorite spectator sport. The national team, called the All Blacks, is one of the best in the world, and its players are considered national heroes. Cricket is the country's oldest organized sport.

Above: Like American baseball, cricket is played with a ball and a bat. Although it is an old game, cricket is still played often in New Zealand.

Boat Racing

Another popular sport in New Zealand is sailboat racing. In 1995 and 2000, New Zealand's team won the most **prestigious** prize in this sport — the America's Cup.

The Maori hold canoe races each year. Their annual river **regatta**, on North Island's Waikato River, attracts people from all over the world.

Above:
Auckland's Annual Yachting Regatta is the largest one-day sailboat race in the world.

Waitangi Day

February 6 is Waitangi Day. It is New Zealand's national holiday, celebrating the signing of the Treaty of Waitangi with cultural and sporting events and a ceremony at a Maori meeting house. Some Maori do not celebrate. They think the treaty hurt their culture.

Provinces and cities celebrate their own anniversary days, too. In rural areas, agricultural and animal shows attract large crowds.

Below:
These boys are riding a steer at an agricultural show in Rotorua. Agricultural shows generally offer sheepshearing and horseback riding demonstrations and contests for the best cakes, jams, and garden vegetables.

Christmas and Other Holidays

For New Zealanders, Christmas comes during the summer, so some families spend the holiday at the beach or take a vacation. Still, they exchange gifts and celebrate with a traditional dinner of lamb or turkey.

April 25 is ANZAC Day. ANZAC, the Australian and New Zealand Army Corps, was formed during World War I.

Below: On December 25, it is summer in New Zealand.

Above: Men show their strength in a wood-chopping competition near the coastal town of Invercargill.

On April 25, 1915, thousands of ANZAC soldiers fought and died in the Battle of Gallipoli in Turkey. The parades and ceremonies held on ANZAC Day honor the soldiers who served in World War I and in the wars that followed.

Other holidays in New Zealand include New Year's Day, Good Friday, Easter Monday, the Queen's Birthday, Labour Day, Boxing Day, and Guy Fawkes Day.

Food

Lamb is a very popular food in New Zealand. Along with beef, lamb is part of a favorite dish — the meat pie, which is usually served with potatoes, peas, and gravy. Steak and sausages are popular foods for barbecues.

The oceans around New Zealand provide many kinds of seafood, from cod to oysters. Fish and chips is a common take-out food.

Below: New Zealanders enjoy a wide variety of fruits and seafoods.

Pavlova is a favorite New Zealand dessert. It is a meringue cake covered with whipped cream and fresh fruit.

Maori Cooking

At Maori feasts, many foods are made in a *hangi* (HAH-nyee), or earth-oven. The food is cooked on stones laid over a fire that is built in a pit. *Kumara* (koo-MAH-rrah) and ***muttonbird*** is a special Maori dish that is cooked in a hangi.

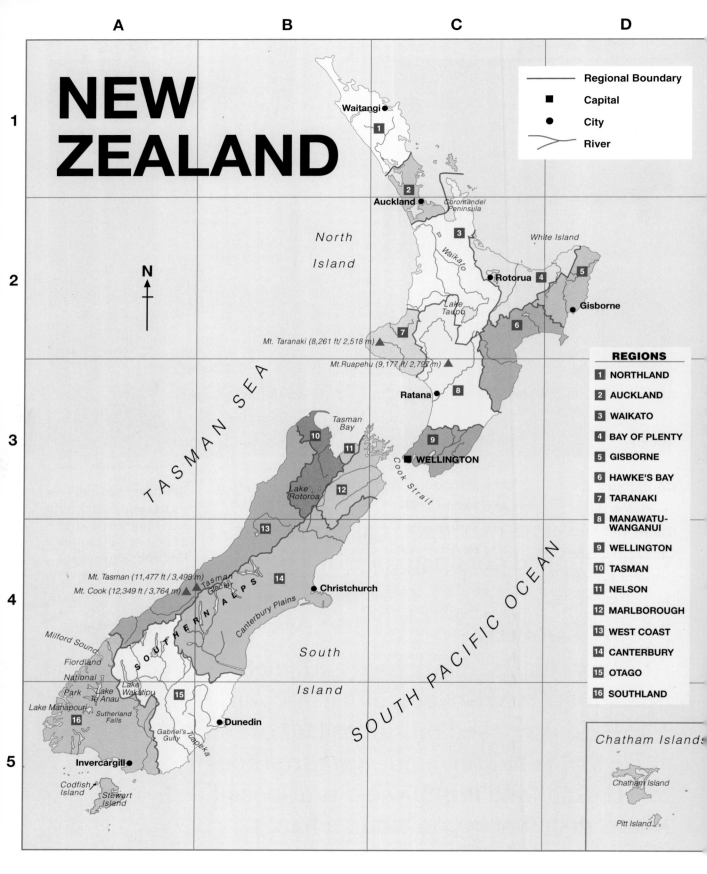

NEW ZEALAND

A B C D

1

2

3

4

5

—	Regional Boundary	
■	Capital	
●	City	
~	River	

Waitangi ●

1

2

Auckland ●

North

Island

N

Coromandel Peninsula

3

Waikato

White Island

Rotorua ● **4**

5

2

Gisborne ●

Lake Taupo

6

Mt. Taranaki (8,261 ft/ 2,518 m) ▲ **7**

Mt. Ruapehu (9,177 ft/ 2,797 m) ▲

Ratana ● **8**

TASMAN SEA

Tasman Bay

10 **11**

9

■ WELLINGTON

Cook Strait

12

Lake Rotoroa

13

Mt. Tasman (11,477 ft / 3,498 m)

Mt. Cook (12,349 ft / 3,764 m) ▲ ▲ *Tasman Glacier*

14

Christchurch ●

SOUTHERN ALPS

Canterbury Plains

South

Island

Milford Sound

Fiordland

National

Park

Lake Te Anau

Lake Wakatipu

15

Lake Manapouri

16

Sutherland Falls

Gabriel's Gully

Tuapeka

Dunedin ●

SOUTH PACIFIC OCEAN

Invercargill ●

Codfish Island

Stewart Island

REGIONS

1	NORTHLAND
2	AUCKLAND
3	WAIKATO
4	BAY OF PLENTY
5	GISBORNE
6	HAWKE'S BAY
7	TARANAKI
8	MANAWATU-WANGANUI
9	WELLINGTON
10	TASMAN
11	NELSON
12	MARLBOROUGH
13	WEST COAST
14	CANTERBURY
15	OTAGO
16	SOUTHLAND

Chatham Islands

Chatham Island

Pitt Island

Above: Most of the sheep farms in New Zealand are small family farms.

Auckland C2

Canterbury
   Plains B4
Chatham Island D5
Chatham Islands D5
Christchurch B4
Codfish Island A5
Cook Strait C3
Coromandel
   Peninsula C1–C2

Dunedin B5

Fiordland National
   Park A4–A5

Gabriel's Gully A5
Gisborne D2

Invercargill A5

Lake Manapouri A5
Lake Rotorua B3
Lake Taupo C2
Lake Te Anau A5
Lake Wakatipu A5

Milford Sound A4
Mt. Cook A4
Mt. Ruapehu C3
Mt. Taranaki C2
Mt. Tasman A4–B4

North Island B1–C3

Pitt Island D5

Ratana C3
Rotorua C2

South Island A5–C3
South Pacific
   Ocean C5–D4
Southern Alps
   A4–B4
Stewart Island A5
Sutherland Falls A5

Tasman Bay B3

Tasman Glacier B4
Tasman Sea A3–B2
Tuapeka River
   A5–B5

Waikato River C2
Waitangi C1
Wellington C3
White Island C2

Quick Facts

Official Name	New Zealand
Capital	Wellington
Official Languages	English and Maori
Population	3.8 million
Land Area	103,737 square miles (268,680 square km)
Major Islands	North Island, South Island
Major Cities	Auckland, Christchurch, Wellington
Highest Point	Mount Cook 12,349 feet (3,764 m)
Longest River	Waikato River (North Island)
Largest Lake	Lake Taupo (North Island)
Ethnic Groups	European (75 percent), Maori (10 percent), Pacific Islander (4 percent), Asian and others (11 percent)
Important Holidays	Waitangi Day (February 6)
	ANZAC Day (April 25)
	Guy Fawkes Day (November 5)
	Christmas Day (December 25)
Currency	New Zealand dollar (NZ $2.30 = U.S. $1 in 2001)

Opposite: This Maori boy is trying to look fierce as he holds a spear in a traditional war dance.

Glossary

advent: arrival or beginning.

bills: proposed laws that government representatives discuss and vote on.

constellation: a group of stars that forms a pattern in the sky and is often given a name.

converted: changed from one belief or faith to another.

crater: a bowl-shaped hole or hollow at the top of a volcano.

descent: family background or heritage.

discrimination: the unfair treatment of certain people based on their race, religion, or ethnic background.

extinction: the state of having died out as a species.

fjords: narrow strips of sea between steep cliffs along a coastline.

glaciers: large masses of ice that move very slowly down a mountain.

habitat: an animal's natural home.

immigrants: people who leave their home country to live permanently in another country.

marae (mah-rah-EE): the sacred area in front of a traditional meeting house.

minority: a group of people with a different racial, religious, or cultural background from most of the other people in a particular country.

muttonbird: any of several species of ocean birds found in Australia and New Zealand.

mythology: a collection of legends and fables, of a particular people or society, that has been passed down through history.

polytechnics: schools that teach technical subjects, such as industrial arts and applied sciences.

predators: animals that hunt and kill other animals for food.

prestigious: well-known and respected.

prospectors: people who explore an area looking for gold or other valuable natural resources.

regatta: a boat race or an event that includes a series of boat races.

terrain: the physical appearance of an area of land.

Union Jack: the name of Great Britain's national flag.

More Books to Read

Australia and New Zealand.
   Elaine Landau (Children's Press)

*A Home by the Sea: Protecting Coastal
   Wildlife.* Kenneth Mallory
   (Gulliver Books)

*Land of the Long White Cloud:
   Maori Myths, Tales, and Legends.*
   Kiri Te Kanawa (Pavilion)

Laz Goes to New Zealand.
   Peggy Smith (Vantage Press)

Maori. Robert MacDonald (Raintree/
   Steck-Vaughn)

Maui and the Sun: A Maori Tale. Gavin
   Bishop (North-South Books)

The Moas. Katie Beck.
   (Landmark Editions)

New Zealand. Pat Ryan (Child's World)

New Zealand. Cultures of the World
   series. Roselynn Smelt
   (Benchmark Books)

*New Zealand. Enchantment of the
   World* series. Mary Virginia Fox
   (Children's Press)

New Zealand. Festivals of the World
   series. Jonathan Griffiths
   (Gareth Stevens)

New Zealand in Pictures. Department
   of Geography (Lerner)

Videos

*Anyplace Wild: Trekking and
   Climbing in New Zealand.*
   (PBS Home Video)

New Zealand. (IVN Entertainment)

*New Zealand and the South Pacific
   Islands.* (Library Video)

Web Sites

maori.org.nz/s_show/

teacher.scholastic.com/glokid/zealand/

www.kcc.org.nz

www.nzrugby.com

Due to the dynamic nature of the Internet, some web sites stay current longer than
others. To find additional web sites, use a reliable search engine with one or more
of the following keywords to help you locate information about New Zealand.
Keywords: *Auckland, kiwi, Maori, marae, Mount Cook, Waitangi, Wellington.*

Index